Mary & the Giant Mechanism

"Riven by the events of the first decade of this century and shot through with grief and a bird-like wonder, Mary Molinary uses the space of the poetry collection to experiment with a form—and therefore invent a mechanism—to reckon with this 'marked little bird of a heart' that must live each day with the knowledge of the ongoing torture, war, and violence performed in one's name. Perhaps in imitation of a complicity alternately figurative and real, the poet situates commonplaces hard by the nearly indescribable: a borrowed ornithology joined to an ancient illumination, 'a speaking self' beside 'a seen other,' elegy followed by apology followed by 'what will emerge.' Through her thousand fresh images and tender elisions we are asked to look and finally see. To read *Mary & the Giant Mechanism* is to revisit our common history with an open, lyric heart."
— *Carol Ann Davis, judge's citation for the Tupelo Press First Book Award*

"Early in *Mary & the Giant Mechanism*, the poet-speaker acknowledges, 'my whole life there's been war in warmer places.' Comprised almost entirely of two long sequences, Mary Molinary's brilliant first book is, among other things, a meditation on the American wars in Iraq and Afghanistan. 'Form carries its own disclosure' Molinary asserts, prompting us to consider her own formal choices: syntax marked by fragmentation and elision, often rendering thought incomplete or indeterminate and putting pressure on her startling images (drawn from disciplines as diverse as particle physics, painting, anthropology, and ornithology) to accrete meaning. . . . The poet-speaker struggles with the book's overriding concern: whether or not it is possible to be *aware* of ongoing terror—how, if 'we cannot or dare not see the truest things,' do we ever truly 'see'? Given the paradoxical nature of the problem, these poems cannot fully answer their own questions. Nonetheless, Molinary suggests that something other than violence tethers individuals across vast geo-political positions to each other—the desire to 'prepare the cell we have in common,' to 'sing your secret bird to sleep.'"
—*Shara McCallum*

"To stop time is one of the most powerful aspects of literary art, especially lyrical poetry in its 'silence and slow time.' In the long sequence 'The book of 8:38,' Mary Molinary brings us repeatedly to an examination of a particular moment of the day, 'Each minute a form / Each one / leading another on.' Is time actually linear as it goes round and round? The second hand 'stammers,' as each second the clock ('*chunk*') punches itself in the face. The immediacy of time, its fleeting 'now' as lyric, meets with an epic simultaneity of experience. Yet knowledge of time is also awareness of your role in time: 'But 8:38 gathers up // the water of me & holds / me captive in a small bowl // Measures me out all night / Makes the stone of me watch.' I admire this absorbing, witty, and often beautiful work."
— *Paul Hoover*

The Tupelo Press First Book Award

Jennifer Michael Hecht, *The Last Ancient World*
Selected by Janet Holmes

Aimee Nezhukumatathil, *Miracle Fruit*
Selected by Gregory Orr

Bill Van Every, *Devoted Creatures*
Selected by Thomas Lux

David Petruzelli, *Everyone Coming Toward You*
Selected by Campbell McGrath

Lillias Bever, *Bellini in Istanbul*
Selected by Michael Collier

Dwaine Rieves, *When the Eye Forms*
Selected by Carolyn Forché

Kristin Bock, *Cloisters*
Selected by David St. John

Jennifer Militello, *Flinch of Song*
Megan Snyder-Camp, *The Forest of Sure Things*
Daniel Khalastchi, *Manoleria*
Mary Molinary, *Mary & the Giant Mechanism*
Each selected by Carol Ann Davis and Jeffrey Levine

Mary & the Giant Mechanism

Mary Molinary

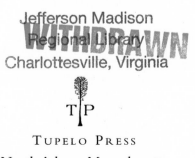

TUPELO PRESS

North Adams, Massachusetts

Mary & the Giant Mechanism
Copyright 2013 Mary Molinary. All rights reserved.

Library of Congress Cataloging-in-Publication Data

Molinary, Mary Helen, 1961–
[Poems. Selections]
Mary & the Giant Mechanism : Poems / Mary Molinary. -- First paperback edition.
    pages cm. — (Tupelo Press Annual First Book Award)
Includes bibliographical references.
ISBN 978-1-936797-23-3 (paperback original : alk. paper)
I. Title. II. Title: Mary and the Giant Mechanism.
PS3613.O456A6 2013
811'.6--dc23

2013022816

Cover and text designed by Howard Klein.
Cover: "Bird With Egg," by Morris Graves (1910–2001); from a double-sided drawing, graphite on paper,
8 x 9.5 inches. Photographed by Marcia Glover. Used with permission of (and thanks to) the Morris Graves
Foundation, by courtesy of the gallery Seattle ArtREsource (www.seattleartresource.com/).

First paperback edition: August 2013.

Printed in the United States.

Tupelo Press
P.O. Box 1767
243 Union Street, Eclipse Mill, Loft 305
North Adams, Massachusetts 01247
Telephone: (413) 664-9611 / Fax: (413) 664-9711
editor@tupelopress.org / www.tupelopress.org

Tupelo Press is an award-winning independent literary press that publishes fine fiction, nonfiction, and poetry
in books that are a joy to hold as well as read. Tupelo Press is a registered 501(c)3 nonprofit organization, and
we rely on public support to carry out our mission of publishing extraordinary work that may be outside the
realm of the large commercial publishers. Financial donations are welcome and are tax deductible.

scolopendra scolopendra

Contents

I

Now the hour bows down, it touches me, throbs …

—Rilke, from *The Book of Hours*

Then I came entire to this moment …

—Rukeyser, from "Breaking Open"

The book of 8:38

Small parts slowly at work   —vivid automata—   a second-hand stammers
          round a clock face   a nervous child
                    casting   shadows   as   it   goes   round   &
          round   in   mimicry   of   itself   of   a   linear   thing.

          Digital clocks cast no shadows   therefore   like the shades whom Dante
                    encounters   in Purgatory   no Matter.   Clocks with hands
          Now   that's another story.   Each minute a form.   Each one

                    leading another on.   8:38   for example   & 38 seconds!
          A chance minute.   A Previously   merging into   an Afterwards.
          A juncture in which   one   must   be   willing.   An imperceptible shift
                    of light on   any object it strives to illumine.

          Any book of hours hides in it   a diary of minutes   a volume   (a reading)   of days.
          A season   its feasts.
          Among its *am*'s & *pm*'s   Winter hunkers speechless against
                    any given minute   its birth   —rushing.   Fallen.

Cold. A cold to quiet all things. Cold as fruit. Cold for anywhere—
especially so for a city in the South. 5 small Clementine oranges
arranged in front of me, imported from Spain (via Puerto Rico?).
On the radio I'm told Florida oranges & other produce are in grave
danger—must be early-plucked. Severe cold snap. Because of arctic
wind, the heaters won't work. I'm only mildly worried about scurvy.
But my whole life there's been war in warmer places. Outside is dark.
Oil-dark, enemy-dark. Mechanical like minutes.

Minutes like this, tempered to 10 degrees Fahrenheit or lower:
the shades of their hands can appear to be brief possessions by clarity.

99% of the time, what was passed between men was a token of time—a watch.

90% of the watches passed in such manner were pocket-watches (in movies on TV in real life). Keepers of Time. Keepers of Order. In real life on TV in movies, time meant something else for women ... I know this sounds simple but Fathers & Grandfathers have never taken to alarm clocks—one sees examples of this everywhere. (Attached to the pocket-watch there *are* rights & privileges which cling to the chain like graveyards). There is one pocket-watch in this house & it stopped years ago. All other time-pieces around here are tired, seek reinvention.

In the simple technology of this 8:38 *am* nothing but sun on its winterly-southerly route makes definitions through the windows.

Should have seen this square jaw coming.

Should have seen this Keeper of Order. This cold winter.

Should have listened to the almanac of squirrels which back in October had all the trees picked clean of nuts. Should have seen this cold eye etched in the bark. Each form (trees, their keepers) carries its own disclosure. Each form carries a miniature of its own destruction. Much the same as this 8:38—seeing this in that. Much the same as the way any given minute can become disconsolate & then a destruction to its own Myth. & now it's Time to punch the clock. Somewhere, not here, the minute is not 8:38 & yet the clock (*kh-chunk*) is punched just the same. Just the same, the shift (a shift) begins.

    Like some ridiculous dawn downing its own invention in shafts of cold & light.
    Oh the terrible engine-birds are not asleep

(Do all poems say the same thing?)

could this minute be the same as any other—caught
in the infinitude of its own outline—an eight
on its side?　　(∞)
infinite as mollusk. wave. mollusk.
& somehow free?

you　　oh stammerer
oh yet-to-be born
among things
you simply will have
to say

How we inhabit this same space secretly
  thrills me. Like Einstein. Time's
  little algorithms of glint & possibility. No doubt
  8:38 exists & you sit now on its sturdy lap.
  Oh it has a skinny shadow. Oh
  it is nitrogen fleeing the scene of a crime.
  8:38 holds in its hands the synchronicity
  of our correspondence. Alchemies of coffee steam
  rising from our cups. What I see
  in the gesture of your hands as they wave in the night.

What the birds only think they understand.

Faced with 8:38 (its form & function,
  its deliberate countenance) anything I could say turns
  cheap & aphoristic.   Blush & stumble words
  armored in intent.

  My time spent (spine bent) in the brevity of
  this 8:38—in the linger & lull of its quick arms
  —has been Auspicious.   A piece of luck.
  & Opportune.

  Because time can instruct. Is.
  Is always, in a sense, 8:38 & never
  a finished thing.   Time is becoming (tense
  & aspect) less rigid or more so.

  Any form tends to become its own
  function & carries within it (clutched
  or cradled)   a miniature of its own
  destruction.

  Movement & form are not the same
  thing unless movement is given form
  (is formed by   & accepts
  the gesture).

  What have I done?   (for example)

  My eyes opened just as the bedroom
  clock (digital) configured as if on ice 8:38.
  Day, thus far, appears   convex & not
  altogether unpleasant.

Strangers exchange gifts.
    Same as anyone else.
    Scented candles.
    Books of verse.

    Tonight the relationships are clear.
    8:38 & I exchange glances.

    In the kitchen now the only sound is
    The second-hand's tiny click as it makes
    Ready the minutes: Loops forward & slips
    Back into nothing.

Given a theory of miniatures, 8:38
    is a weapon of mass destruction & to be feared.

    once we feared the atom bomb, alone. now,
    as then, the most dangerous things are small:

    the self hiding in humanism.
    the miniature flame hidden in the wood.
    the 2 tiny voids in an 8.

8:38 has begun
      to hang about with a certain
      & alarming ease. Entering the kitchen

      just now, I saw it
      unpack a bag. Heard it
      say under-the-breath, almost singing

          things ain't half
          bad 'round here,
          think I might
          stay put a li'l while

On us too

    beings & things
    cast no shadow
    morning is slim
    sunless & nervous
    a minute belies me
    a minute betrays
    a hand's tiniest
    hesitation

    in this kitchen
    now
    toast toasting in a toaster
    & time's utter
    refusal to obey
    the promise of its own
    consistency, its own
    myth

    as if planning
    already
    the daily, the small
    celebrations
    kept secret & to itself

    while I have   coffee & toast
    8:38 prefers   tea & eggs

Good

to see you again!

(lies. lies. lies.)

8:38 is clearly
misanthrope
some days wants
to slip by
unnoticed & un-noted
wants to be
indistinguishable from 8:36, 10:20, the train
lowing in the distance, off canvas
& out of focus.

8:38 enjoys solitude
seeing
a movie alone.

I've heard stories, been told that
on occasion
8:38 has been known
to burrow deep
into the darkness of matter.

8:38 is a varmint scratching in the night walls.

Last night: 4 poets in a room
       Mary said that she is tired of poems
       Tired of reading them
       Tired of making them
       Perhaps, she went on,
       I am tired of life now
       Had my say
       Knit   sewn   knit
       Cross-stitched
       A number of lives here
       Then her lips kept moving but
       The only sound in that room
       Of 4 poets was 8:38—perched on
       Her tongue & fashioning there a loom
       On the loom all the poems
       As yet unwritten

The most dangerous things are small …

    miniature flame hiding in the wood …

    3 specks united in ellipsis …

    interruption … fade-out … or … what's not said …

    who does not know by now

    what minutiae hang on the blind minute

    hand as it begins its ascent

    up from 8:38 on the circle that is not round …

    but clamors just the same …

Eight thirty eight is a travelogue & past
      we were: SW of Ruidoso, NM (outerest
      edge of Apache Reservation)
      there were:
      horses & orchards & fruit stands &
      a bank with a digital clock out front:
      perpetual relationship of
      Time & Temp: (a matter of degrees)
      52°F   8: ( ) 8
      on constant display with the one light out
      so the thirty is implied by the absence of
      numeral 3 & one can, in that space left,
      sense the contingency of one's situation—
      stripped away like that
      2 Arabic 8's
      (in mild weather hired to hold down
      the Fort of Commerce) appear alembic, yes,
      but ludicrous standing like proud soldiers guarding
      the missing 3—the *no* implied in the hollow.

What I have not told you:
    The kitchen wall clock has neither
    Roman nor Arabic numerals—nor
    does it have blank spaces (the fashion
    for a while when we knew perfectly well
    what was meant by the spaces). This clock
    was seen on TV. Has birds instead of numbers.

        song sparrow: house wren song sparrow

    Please go back & replace all pertinent
    references with birds. 8:38 falls just south
    of song sparrow (male), north of American
    robin (male). Such clocks sing only on the hour.

8:38 is pumice & ceramic
    ashen-faced & staring

    me down across the table
    We've been like this

    for so long now I must be
    stone   rubbed smooth

    by the minuscule oceans
    pouring having poured from

    my eyes & having formed
    (been formed by)

    estuary & rivulet
    contingency   *contingency*

    I must want it to say
    over & over   again & again

    But 8:38 does not even say that
    Will not utter even that word from

    that crooked smile flanked by those
    4 dry sockets   *8:38!*

    I command with all
    the seriousness of stone

    Leave this place at once
    But 8:38 gathers up

    the water of me & holds
    me captive in a small bowl

measures me out all night
makes the stone of me watch

8:38 greets me like a volume:

> familiar & carried around
> since birth. Accumulating.

> Just because something (music, say) is
> able to be expressed in numbers
> does not mean that numbers exist.

> 8:38, as I've told you, expresses
> itself with no more than a sigh
> or a click. A shadow or drop

> of water. On the Hour, however, a bird will sing.

> *January 31st is an inheritance*
> *as are all the days months years given*
> *Proper Names. All Proper Names*

> *are inherited* says 8:38 as it puts on leather
> shoes, tells me it will soon be leaving
> to make a pilgrimage to a place

> where each minute has its own
> Proper Name. As much as I want
> it to go, instead I hear myself say

> > *Don't be silly. The volume is not*
> > *yet full. Besides, you haven't even*
> > *finished your tea & eggs.*

> *If you stay, you can have a name.*
> …
> 8:38 is so quiet it seems no longer

in the kitchen, but elsewhere,
tumbling through the volume
of itself. Barely nodding, then,

& staring off into space, 8:38 replies
maybe. maaaybeeee (holding
that *a* & final *e* in interrogative uplift)

& shall we name them? & will
they have their own purple cups?

8:38 is straw
      light—a slant & sleight
      tilt of metamorphoses.

      8:38 is o-
      verheard argument
      amidst cinder & concrete.

      8:38 is a
      lover's despera-
      tion. 8:38 does not

      exist except in the
      telling by objects
      as they tremolo through space.

      8:38 is what
      we tell ourselves in
      consolation, grief. Perhaps,

      reconciliation.
      No one or number
      is awake enough to fight

      & mean it, but in this
      mean time of this year,
      8:38 feels its strength,

      hangs heavy from morning's
      rafters, seems to *shift*,
      lifts a lip & prods us on.

According to Ovid, all relationships are
    clear & figurative. Details, a small bit
    of truth. In his version of "Arachne," for
    example, the violence on her tapestry:
    threads, details appear as bland as any 8:38
    when held away from the others. A microcosm.

According to Ovid, Minerva's beautiful
punishments in miniature seem nearly natural.
Questioning leads only to trouble.

            Wait. ...   (empires favor story?)

According to Ovid, Arachne's tapestry unveils
Minerva's—thread by bloody thread.   Trouble.
Arachne's punishment is brutal & far from *natural*   (no
work of art can presume to contain *all* of it).
Thus is she left: a small austere life of finely spun
minutes, details amounting to no   meaning:
to infinite   interpretations.

No figurative art allowed.   Wait.   ... (abstract art favors empires?)

        What are you trying to tell me?

8:38 is a flat place with a cold February wind.
>A small town in Arkansas where
>some people have lived for nearly one hundred
>years & others come back to be buried.

>8:38 is an unfinished pine box atop straps—
>a vault awaiting it because vaults are Health Code.
>Viruses (like stories & time) do not die. Can seep out.

>8:38 is a memory—a moving away from
>8:38 is a memory—a moving away from
>Mississippi in 1925.

>8:38 is a migration.   A bollweevil.

8:38 can't help but believe in
    Reincarnation—a repetition
    of forms—pre-existing
    forms always to be dealt with.

    8:38 told me that the 21st
    century will be not unlike the 20th
    what with its 8:38s following
    its 8:37s & all the stories

    those with Names have told one
    another to make themselves feel
    better. 8:38 went on & on about epic time
    & the different generations & their

    stories & ended by saying *Read*
    their books. See their movies. 8:38
    laughed in such a way that revealed
    to me, in slow & certain detail,

    the face of a god—a history
    of heavenly crimes
    collecting like foam in the corners
    of its sadistic grin.

To illuminate a Book of Hours, a small prayer

Book for private devotion, was nothing new.

But the brothers Limbourg, circa 1415, painted

Miniature scenes of daily life under the rule of:

Constellations, seasons, dukes.

All accounts show that brothers & duke all died

The same year of the same plague.

Illuminations incomplete.

      [Please illustrate this book—its margins.

      Put there drolleries or daily

      Life. Small feasts. Or

      3 Limbourg brothers & their hours giving way

      To days to seasons

      To an expanse of zodiacs

      That must be made large & kept apart

      From perishable things]

& 8:38 was pacing a path
       back & forth between
       the 6 & 9:

       Those brothers had it
       all wrong it asserts
       Each quarter hour holds
       all the Season one needs.

       & it is all very rhythmic
       & quite tempting to fall
       into the embrace of
       time without history

       until one sees what
       I have seen: 8:38. The tyrant
       marching in calculated step
       holding the minute hand
       like a bullhorn &
       shouting proclamations:
                … boards & thistles! …
                … far too cold! …
                … for no reason, a thousand birds! …
                … abstractions! weeping woman with cup …

Thus does

8:38 hold me hostage in the winter of this kitchen arranging
on the table the distance between coffee & toast & the passing of
hours … & I'm not sorry for having stared into the maw hidden in a slow
blink, my hand full of minutes. 8:38 *reads* me all day, all day I can
tell it *nothing*. But in that space, that ferment, 8:38 seems a lingering
salt, broken against its own gravity. Crammed & caught in a difficult mouth.
Though still marked at its edges with a hardness, 8:38 slowly appears:
a small oblique, a sturdy anointing with oil & nitrogen, a straining to reach
some hour when a bird will sing. & the wall clock becomes a white
paper plate with construction paper hands attached with a brass fastener.
"Frankly," I proclaim, "all I ever wanted was *this*. To learn to read this."
8:38, lithe as ritual, kisses my chill body & mutters   *At last. Alas.*
8:38 begins to hum & its humming distills to words:

> *a pine tree in whose fragrant branches*
> *a nest of birds sings in the moonlight:*
> *birds singing in the moonlight*

"Oh. José Martí," I whisper & then ask, "What are you trying to tell me?"
But 8:38 returns to humming & releases me into the accidental details.

& 8:38 in the costume
of Mendicant went
from the kitchen
out the door
& among the people …

... 8:38 is lacuna & either
    devouring its children or
    multiplying & sunning
    itself like planets—still
    I look for it from time to
    time like some jealous moon

Imagine my surprise upon
    walking in to find
    8:38 sitting at the kitchen
    table in a little hair shirt.

    8:38 is concerned because
    no one would listen:
    Deaf ears. Blind eyes.
    Far too cold.

    I tell 8:38 that perhaps it bemoans being
    domesticated—as would any household god
    or human imposition— & dependent upon
    oblations & sparrow song.

    We decide to stay up all night,
    drink whiskey, discuss reconciliation—
    all possible conjugations
    & virtues of existing.
    & how minutia becomes oppressive.

    We find ourselves at dawn
    laughing often & deeply.

    8:38 decides to stay until spring.

[Please illustrate this page.

Put here drolleries & daily life. Small feasts. A season.]

II

DEATH.   *Everyman, stand still! Whither art thou going thus gaily?*

—Anonymous, from *Everyman* (c.1495)

To walk along the used-up path that narrows, is

necessary.

A burning—back of throat—is not gentle or dull.   All thirst.

Were a stranger here, s/he'd most certainly be

brilliant.

We would rest with the ease of moss. Appear washed in our dreams—
continue relentless as water, clean as precipice.

Hurtled into.

The brilliant stranger said: *We've been lied to by particles pretending*

to be strings … & yet

Strings are divine in their washing.

With what grace they scrub

our heavy slumbering!

Chaste as vinegar we awaken.

The path is long. Humility & Hubris look like dewdrops. Or fruit

perched atop the hard spirits lining the path.

Another stranger approaches. How cramped we are & still

alive.

That night we dreamt: the strangers in their blessedness. I in my thirst.

To demonstrate how serene is sadness, the 2nd stranger sits & unmoving

cries.

The hard spirits are not embarrassed—nor are we. Nothing but a clearing
is articulated in the given gesture of actual grief.

Even our rest is contorted according to grief's narrow contours—to the
uncurtained

hour.

And none here have wallowed in the suffering.

Though, at times, the path does.

III

Birds who does have the feed will hum;
those that isn' got the feed woudn' be able to hum

—Anonymous (attributed to "Coconut Villager")

Bird signs

Preface: bird decembering

A migratory angel of autumn
folded into the much
misunderstood
genome of its organza
wings & perched
atop the dusty corner cupboard:

Tell me your last thoughts
it said.

Said I
Tell me your first.

That's easy
said the angel
I'm flying.

Little known bird of the ribcage

Either 2 birds crossed
The blue air
Just in front of you or

Missiles were prepared
& placed on an X-marked border

Either a quiet morning marked
By blossomings-out &
Smallish vegetables or

The political prisoner
Awakes in the same
Cell with the same

First thought as yesterday

The cell we have in common
The target we share
What you believed once

Still holds: the body
Free or imprisoned

Your bird is your secret
A rod of carbon in an arc
Of light infinitely

Before we were fossils
We were merely

Hungry & chattering
Consequently

There is the body
Free or imprisoned there is
Justice or there is not

Prepare the cell we have in common
Sing your secret bird to sleep

The ribcage is a cage for this
The ribcage is a fine cage for this
Marked little bird of a heart

Archeozoic neolithia / ceremonial bowl taking the shape of a bird

Again the ancestor awakes with in her somewhere a stone

Each morning the stone grinds itself like flint

She gnashes her teeth

Where the stone is, she never knows at first

Some days the stone is a heart-stone, a toe-stone, a bone-stone, and so on

Some days the stone is a fistful of sleep to put in her pocket for later

The stone is   everything true   She is a lie around it

The stone   is   everything   true

The stone is a great liar

The stone could be cracked open in the manner of an egg

Inside the stone is a vast body of water

Inside the stone is a still vaster sky   A desert

Every element present in the body   Every element present at the Big Bang

The stone is a volcano   All up-swell

The stone is a gesture of greeting—2 people on a pathway

The stone never stops singing

The stone never says a word   There are words

All over it & filling it up

– _____ –

Bone meal. Blood meal. Nitrogen & x-number carbon molecules + illuminated manuscripts annotated. A mode of absence. As though this is unencumbered fiction. A journey into. As though this is. Heard as read.

– _____ –

Soon pared down to red maple devoid. Secret gardens or graves. Inhumations under the last remnants of stunning autumn. Sky will appear blue & no. Ink-black branches scraping—scratching at—December.

– _____ –

Take cover. Seek warmth & fire. Heavy snows certain. A disembarrassment of plot. Keep the weak indoors. Woolen figures haunt the white streets.

– _____ –

As though this is. A habit. Snow-melt filling mouths with lambent tributaries. Pared down to mythos & pathos & vowel sounds. That which escapes the body on hardy molecules of carbon dioxide. The dead come gasping up for air.

Oh! where are the bright birds

But for the *varied thrush calling in autumn,*
but for this slight mere breeze, are we not
already posthumous—what we choose when
we choose to walk with the dead
—to invite them in for an orange,
a biscuit, tea—when we implore them
to hear our confession—when we know, know
the dead well enough to know that they prefer

motion—toes articulating, heels lifting in quick
lilt, fingers splayed—feeling fully those slight
mere bones in the feet & in the hands—bones
that make birds of us—fragile & brittler
turning as older we get—we begin as fish—
supple of bone   soft of skull—we begin well

Bird experiencing light

Those mornings in march were fearless   translucent
all honey & nest   dappling & roan
strident queries of crow & whole orchards in bloom

clear to the sky   the sky was just on top of us & powder
blue quelled the gunshot from the hearts of enemies   no one
no thing   was a stranger

tenebrous fish in a makeshift pond   a miniature ravine
when first sun strikes them
together they golden they koi & gleam

Gull floating on a sea of light (we

                              leave the beaches for the tourists, mostly)
                                      Mostly we rummage through
                                              their leavings
                                          mostly we call them
                                                snowbirds
                                            we etch other
                                 names for them in the sea-
                                     glass & sands of other
                                        languages on other
                                 shores (seems some days we were
                                       meant to be theirs,
                                       see, why even fight it)
                             mostly the sun rises & sets like coral
                                              reef fires
                                             & the tides
                                          shift in & out
                                            like mass
                                 migrations of ancient travelers
                                         then can we be
                               found combing the strand, mostly

Dying pigeon series

The first shot is pigeons   rows & rows of pigeon frame by
frame then young soldiers returning   this must be
about common things   *common   things*   the soldiers
all wear strange eyeglasses that turn out
to be microscopes   you too wear strange eyeglasses but your right
lens is a microscope while your left lens is a telescope in this
way you never see things   *as they are* in this way you only see things
as they are   seen this way pigeons contain multitudes & nevertheless are
squab & sometimes   served with squash

That you are hungry even in your sleep does not warrant
interpretation hunger is simple   even if not enough bread some
bread & for some many no bread you do not need special
eyewear to see this   to pretend hunger is complicated is
a crime even in your sleep   hunger is not dragonflies suddenly
disappearing from a marsh or the dying of frogs bread is simple
hunger & dragonflies too   pigeons are simple
for every pigeon a message to be sent
along the lines of erasure into gray–bone empty space
send food & poems

Camera zooms in on single pigeon
the metaphor firmly set   the music
—a purposeful dragging cadence—
sinks down instead of hovering in the air
solidity—even bleakness—to the final cadenza
a frozen light terribly

CROP MILK / STILLS

Patterns of pitch
(as a life seen over time—its hungers &
close-ups   its patterns & amputations)
amounting to a texture

IMBRICATION / EDITS

The first shot is pigeons
a sequence in overlap
shot-roof-birds

DEATH, MOURNING, & PIGEONS

Moving the memorial
statues to a place of safety at the
outset of war   pigeons
disappear   casualties
accumulate   statues lost
forgotten   the pigeons
return to the cities
to roost

Spirit bird (original title: bird resting on the golden stream)

What I know of death is november

Red as virginia creeper & green
As magnolia

Death isn't as quiet as most
Might think

Nor is it a rainstorm

Death has the general shape of a passerine
Just at sundown

Plays among leaves with squirrels & sings
Just because

Death is large & the leaves don't stand
A chance

Nor the stars—oh, the stars—& there
We are

Resting between pantomimes & constellations
On yellow ochre

Streams of moonlight

War maddened bird following St. Elmo's fire

Minuscule germ-birds blew inland on recent hurricanes & began perching
in our bloodstreams
twilight was chalk
we muffled our coughs in white tissues   moist flags of surrender

~

What we cannot or dare not
see may be the truest things

~

Red, it's true, eye see you everywhere these days or expect to
eye follow the blue-green complimentary field the phosphorescent fire of you

~

Early autumn winds, like *words,*
spoken with force gather particles

~

Gather then limn

~

A low applause of senescent
green
leaves as a few begin
their fall   & fall in turns
~

What we or where we inhabit may be
too devastating, you know, under this canopy
thick as it is as green as sea-glass   Sunlight penetrating
nonetheless   Yet less realized

~

Today without doubt a jade wind
turned

Toward the fine teeth of leaves biting at morning
sun—eye note this   Think of you as eye often do
Enamored

~

The mature thyme—a veritable snarl of nature
& history & something mildly medicinal

Amidst cathedrals of basil   let's not be quiet
let's turn our probable faces into it—into
this hue & wind, this early autumnal
moving with the quick pace of a young couple
new to the unknown streets

~

Red

~

Final flames of unnamed flowers fading to gases &, Red,
all of us gases held in containers measured in half-lives
or inches or stanzas

> *A solitary woman! and she went*
> *singing and gathering flower after flower,*
> *with which her way was painted and besprent*
>
> —from Shelley's translation
> of Dante's "Matilda Gathering Flowers"

She pays no mind, she gathers. *This is beauty this is beauty* she chants like hard wood. So then I gather & You gather but He She It gathers. They gather. While we gather well what holds small fires, burns our eyes. I understand as well that certain birds will gather themselves like constellations & fly across a large body of water twice a migratory year (what kinds of birds I think I know). Such flights take days & days upon days & the birds never stop until they reach autumn roost or spring (summer or winter, twice per annum times always over blooms of salt & water to simply gather & nest). They gather & nest.

Brief calligraphies curling-up from the fertile syllogism underfoot. She discerns so many parts per million & the solitary woman finds herself suddenly in revelations of gathering: among teeth & truth: the way a Body records Experience: a noun to its verb & so on. All possible calculations in these fields of singy-singing bone. Of gen gical teeth clicking away, telling tales with ridge & indentation: here was fever, here hunger, here suffering. Here the tooth grew long. Here it did not. Gathered like this, teeth will tell you. But gathered like *this*: rooted in gum, cajoled by tongue, air passing over & through them like a breeze: a field wild with nasturtium.

Chances are: what happens after this is only human. Chances are: what happens after this is fragrant & watercolor & perched near the edges of bold dark lines. Metaphors gathering. Likewise: what happens after this is only human.

When 40 days with no rain but ineluctable twilight
When deep sounds throaty as a nightjar
When the winds mount their ghost-horses
When the mesquite trees tremble
When in the sparse trees' nightening branches
Silhouettes of birds' breath—a breathing visible to a passing eye
When a final horizontal heave of sun thins deepens descends
When then the first star
When then the second
When without variation all stars appear exact
When where we expect & when
When we are sewn to the same stars
When the predictable seems more miraculous than the anomalous
When without warnin spare beans on the bean trees
Rattle their small dry prayers

Thus are there but so many bones in a foot or hand

Thus do they break in degrees

Thus did simple moonlight fuel paranoia

Thus were the wrong battles fought

Thus was commerce & trade

Thus did we bury our shame shallow & our dead deep

Thus did *torture* enter the common tongue & pop culture like a yawn

Thus was nevertheless a bird heard unseen in the weeping willow

Thus a cool breeze at precisely 9:22 *pm* on the 8th day

Thus did we number & count nouns & casualties

Thus will the unseen bird continue its song

Thus will a new moon rise

Thus will an unseen breeze

Thus will the hand & foot

Thus will the graves

Thus will the book

Bird maddened by sound of machinery in the air

[Slightly hunched at the shoulders, head dropped, a four-chambered heart paces the stage. Stops center. Spins, arms out, turns face up to the false dome of sky. The chorus, perched on scaffolding approximating trees, speaks in brief italics.]

> *So here is Tiresias.*
> *At the crossroads. All ventricle*
> *and ululation, conflagration*
> *and gears. See him—cuk cuk cuk!*
> *Feet dancing circles in the sand,*
> *arms out like wings, looking back,*
> *translating …*

[Heart resumes pacing. Speaks out loud, though somewhat pained.]

I could have said—done—*nothing* and they'd have blinded me still. Applied the breasts, removed the breasts. Would still've vanquished my voice to stalk the future in the language of birds.

And I don't mind so much the *ti-dee'-di-di, per-chik-o-ree* of see-sooth-saying, or even the deep and slow *oong-ka-choonks* of justice. I've grown accustomed to the *kree-eet*-ing screams, the futile *chit-chit che* of tragedy. But. I am through

playing to these gods, staying ahead of their slick maneuverings and incessant juvenilia, their muddled voice-ings in the dark.
Quok! Quoi! Quark!

too-i tu whit! A dissonant chord …
a discordant noise … outside, inside.
Dignified Tiresias! Blind
Tiresias. Snake Killer! Who
you? Coyo'te? Legba? Show us
the space between ritual
and reality. Feet!
Feet! Dance circles!

[Heart sounds a sustained high-pitched whistle.]

Because something
smaller than words on air
passes from chicken to human,
the slaughter of the birds has begun!

Doomed chorus, don't think I haven't considered flight—the arc and hard
machinations of wing. Futurity, I tell you the suicides are gathering
in my skirts. Monstrous History. And you, who need … *konk-ah-reee* …
you may see me on your dirty city streets moving between

austerity and the nave of dusk, barely illuminated—for a moment
you won't be certain of my gender—illusionary me. *Poeep-pueep*!
You won't be certain of my genus or species—the quick
unsure bird you may hear and never see …

ca-ha ca-ha, Tiresias must choose!
So who So who has the beak now
that can reach the startled
bugs in the bark?

… *trill-true-eet*   *tse tse tse*   I stand here and, fairly hairless
among you, suspect it is not me … Feel my nose—its obvious
lack of hook. How soft it is and useless.

[Heart resumes spinning, recedes into the shadows of the trees.]

Then fold feather into ready ink

Then a drowsy eye

Then our inconsequential selves

Then *bury them & keep quiet*

Then elegy then apology then what will emerge

Then what is possible resembles free fall or flight

Then that any of this is possible dispels determinacy

Then the hands gone then the thumbs can do no harm

Then strands of continuities / filaments of continuing

Then prehensile nostalgia

Then what can it mean to be idiopathic & interstitial

Then trade acquaintances & valuable objects

Then *reason & the angel of militancy*

Then the body executes itself

Then take the wind in one mouth & expel it from the other

Then a body leads itself / is taken / *el cuerpo*

Then the prohibition of scattered flower petals

Then scatter them

Then beckon with a wing

Then the prohibition of scattered words

Then scatter them

Birds with seeds (possessions)

When wren
fly from a dying

mouth: erasure
but never silence

wingbeat wingbeat
(pbruu pbruu) plus

a clearing of tiny
avian throats

(trill-true-eet) as
they exit

quick-as-poems
one-by-one

the sternum of
the newly dead & take

their places
in the hearts of sharp

skeletal trees
or clamber onto air

currents they will
ride like eloping lovers

~

When wren
flee a dying mouth:

what's left is nest
for lucky

passers-by
during a sudden down-

pour who foldnuzzle
into the shelteringmuzzle

while singing
slightly off-

key like a self-
portrait with possessions

~

The possessions are seeds

~

I have seen this twice

In this picture all movement is around fixed points:

In this picture a speaking self, a seen other:
An illusion of freedom is played:
In this one great glass cities:
An individual rubs the cities with salt:
Pushes them to dissolve:

In this picture a thatched-roof vernacular:
Things we have in common:
Things we have dug up:
An enlarged detail from the Ghent altarpiece is unaccountable:

In this picture most compelling are the motions implied:
The way the chair has only just been pushed away:
The way the background stands in relation:
Even the horizon takes on posture:
As obstinate as icon:
Eternally akimbo:
Both hands on hips:
Elbows outward turned:

IV

... a body rolls down, a nameless / thing, a fallen number ...

—Neruda, from "United Fruit Co."

Whether the birds will awaken is still uncertian.

—Inger Christensen, from *it*

(*vox*) (*memoria*)

Between the sternal murmurs & pernicious amnesia   a bird nests in the throat   Yellow
    & possibly canary

Even when one can *see* the atoms—tinted methyl green & leaning like Athena *away from*—
    comparisons are inevitable

For each copper shield or coin emblazoned   a pair of leather shoes   a scroll
    An alphabet to be exchanged on a cellular level   & along trade routes

An ancestor who was to have formed that part of the backbone holding head to shoulder
    was tyrannized to such degree that one must have to hand enough red ochre always

If you must know   Memory is epileptic as any proton   When memory *is* still   the body
    seizes   A vapor forms face-down on a tongue

An intersection between Matter & Art—call it *pituitary*   after all   to touch the soft   the
    glandular   parts of any surface is no less molecular   No less a transfer of memory of *oh!*

A voice   no   many voices have gathered me   as up with gladness   I now show
    signs of pitch & genetic embellishment

Particular pictures lodged in my chromosomes & stayed there   yearly mutating   Neither
    forlorn nor tumor   really   One must fancy that we call these *poems*   (perched   ready)

What moves me toward memory   then   is neither sealed   nor apocryphal   Is desire
    Is celebrated   (probable   marvelous)   Molecules thick as muscles
        emancipating the mere appearance of feather & skin   …   Listen

There is never
    just one bird hidden in any given throat

. . .

Notes

The book of 8:38. Winter, 2003. Already in Afghanistan, the U.S. prepares its occupation of Iraq while others die at home of viruses, poverty, and other natural causes. Both are largely unseen wars.

Setting out to look for a motif. Spring / Summer, 2003. Dedicated to the memory of J. Douglas Canfield and all of the anonymous dying and dead to come.

Bird signs. Autumns, ~2003–2008. This series began as an attempt to "count" the years of imperial wars in Afghanistan and Iraq. (The series continues, transmogrified into the "Dead Leah" poems.)

Many titles are taken from, or are variations on, painting titles of Morris Graves (1910–2001). These are not ekphrastic poems, however; rather, the poems are in conversation with Graves's evocative titles, his restrained palette, and above all, the fulgent symbolism of birds he explores as a reflection of the inner self, but which stand here as sign and cipher of the Dead, the four-chambered heart—that which we have in common—and, perhaps, the birdsong whence our human language.

"War maddened bird following St. Elmo's fire" picks up on the vibration and light left in the wake of Mei-Mei Berssenbrugge's poem, "Red Quiet." In that poem she writes: *words spoken with force gather particles.* Additionally, "If we were birds once" references the titles of paintings by Goya and Robin Savage respectively. "If we were birds once / captions" are captions written for a series of photographs that do not exist.

(vox) (memoria). Summer / Autumn, 2003. After a painting of same title by Robin Savage.

After-words

This isn't war: this is every day

—Jackson Mac Low

Acknowledgments

Versions of these poems have appeared, some in slightly different form or with different titles, in the following journals: *Beloit Poetry Journal*, *Contemporary American Voices*, *Crazyhorse*, *Jellybucket*, *New American Writing*, *New Orleans Review*, *Pindeldyboz*, *Poetry International*, and the *Tupelo Press Poetry Project*, and some reappeared on *Verse Daily* and *Poetry Daily* and in the anthology *Poetry Daily* (Sourcebooks, 2003). Much gratitude to all the editors and readers involved.

Thank you, thank you to Jeffrey Levine and Carol Ann Davis for choosing my manuscript.

Many extra thanks to Jim Schley of Tupelo Press and to Lee Sharkey and John Rosenwald of *Beloit Poetry Journal* whose sharp and thoughtful editing helped determine the final versions of these poems; and to Shara McCallum, Mary Leader, Beth Bishop, Jason Ezell, Debra Gregerman, Melissa Singleton, and Mark Yakich, all early instigators and/or readers.

Finally, let it be noted: to choose poetry is often to risk stability, housing, and health. I have joyously done so but could not have done so without the financial assistance of others who either paid the rent or bills directly on occasion or bought art from R or gave me extra shifts when I needed cash or days off when I needed to write or kept the utility company diverted from cut-off while I went to pay or kept my spirits up, making it possible for us to continue on. Deep thanks to Elizabeth Molinary, Suzanne M. Fjarli, Pam Canfield, Andy Melpolder, John Molinary, Corrie Houle, Sam and Dolores Molinary, Kaki and Billy Burruss, Louise Palazola, Melissa Singleton, Stacy Wright, Mimi Atkinson, Ken Strickland, Jeff Nesin, Nick and Jacob, all the actual and honorary residents of North Belvedere, and the Memphis Art Brigade.

And to R, of course, without whom.

Born and early-reared in Virginia, MARY   MOLINARY moved in 1968 with her family
to Memphis, Tennessee, where as a child   she was living during the now-historic
garbage strike, the assassination of Martin Luther King, and the arrival of National Guard, when
suddenly her city looked like the pictures of Vietnam on the evening news.

Since then she has had many jobs, including college administrator; editor and seller of classified
ads at alternative newsweeklies; greenhouse and nursery worker; housesitter; legal assistant; reader
for the blind; physical therapy assistant — and through it all, bartender and waitress. Knowing
she would be a writer one day, she chose restaurant work early on as a trade that would support
her as she continues to learn as much as possible about being, and about being human, and about
putting that into language. "Maybe it is just the bread-crumbs we leave. We are eye-witnesses,
one and all."

Her education has been "nomadic and incomplete and exciting," and after many forays she
earned a BA in Cultural and Linguistic Anthropology from the University of Arizona and an
MFA from the University of Memphis. She currently lives in Tucson, Arizona.

Other books from Tupelo Press

See our complete backlist at www.tupelopress.org

APR _ - 2014